ON-AIR

ON-AIR

THE GUIDEBOOK TO STARTING A CAREER AS A RADIO PERSONALITY

- A beginner's guide to getting a job *on the air*.
- The best methods of getting your foot in the door fast.
- Valuable *inside* information to attain an on-air position quickly.
- What you must know to start a career as a radio personality.
- Great resource for industry information and job hunting.

By Jack Broady

BVI

On-Air–The Guidebook to Starting a Career as a Radio Personality
Copyright © 2007 Jack Broady
Published by BVI

For further information, please contact:
jack@bvibook.com

Book design by
Arbor Books, Inc.
19 Spear Road, Suite 301
Ramsey, NJ 07446
www.arborbooks.com

Printed in United States of America

On-Air–The Guidebook to Starting a Career as a Radio Personality
Jack Broady
1. Title 2. Author 3.How To/Radio/Media

Library of Congress Control Number: 2007904466
ISBN 10: 0-9797380-0-8
ISBN 13: 978-0-9797380-0-5

*This book is dedicated to Joyce H. Broady,
my supportive mother who was my biggest fan,
my most loyal listener and my inspiration.
In loving memory.*

CONTENTS

FOREWORD

Whether you have been thinking about pursuing a career as a radio personality for years, months or even days, *On Air* will give you an unbelievable advantage in making your dreams a reality. You will get the four most effective methods of getting your foot in the door at a radio station with little to no experience. You will get revealing tactics to apply in getting on the air once you have attained employment. You will receive valuable information on how to get noticed and a specific list of what to learn from your experienced co-workers. You will find out where to focus your efforts and energy to get ahead fast including dos and don'ts. You will learn industry secrets, the most important aspects of the business and how to perform like a pro once you are on the air. You will also get valuable inside information including harsh truths, the Clear Channel effect, the current state of radio, making an air check tape, earning potential, radio lingo, formats and job titles. In addition, we will guide you to the best websites for job openings, industry news and networking opportunities.

On Air was written with the main purpose of giving you proven methods and tactics that thousands of radio personalities have secretly applied to get started and thrive in this business. As we will mention in this book, not all aspects of the business is covered and you will have to take it upon yourself to treat your new job like a training course, learning details and refining your skills with the help of fellow employees after you have read and applied the information in this book.

On Air is packed with the most useful and common knowledge that you must know in order to be taken seriously and sound competent. It also has methods and tactics that are not common knowledge, but inside information to position you for success and quick results. This book is built to take years of trial and error out of your climb to the top and keep you from reinventing the wheel by revealing inside information that all radio personalities know, but you don't. Now you have this information at your fingertips. We hope this finds you well and that you have many years of success and enjoyment in the fun and exciting radio broadcasting industry!

INTRODUCTION

Achieving a career in the radio broadcasting industry could be one of the most fun and exciting jobs you may ever experience. It is well known that most radio DJ's have a great time when they are at work because they love their jobs. Imagine, actually looking forward to going to work everyday!

In case you did not know, some very famous people on TV got started as a radio personality. People like Oprah Winfrey, David Letterman, Jay Thomas, Adam Corolla, Jimmy Kimmel, Carson Daly and Ryan Seacrest all started as radio personalities. There are also some famous TV stars who have found a new home working in radio. People like Danny Bonaduce, Steve Harvey, Ellen DeGeneres and many others.

As you may already know, there are countless benefits to working at a radio station, especially if you are "on the air." Some of these benefits include; free clothes, free food, free CD's, free movies, free concert tickets, free trips and a whole lot of other radio station goods that you should be able to use in one way or another.

I'm sure your first question is, "how much can I make as a radio DJ?" The salaries in the radio industry can vary greatly from one scenario to the next. Just like any career, you will get back what you put in and in the radio industry, it will always depend on three things; *how good you are, who you know and if you have a history of getting good ratings*. The good news is that you can make an enormous salary if you play your cards right. The bad news is that very few DJs are making millions or even hundreds of thousands.

You may have heard that radio personalities make some of their money from doing "personal appearances." This *is* true and appearances can more than double your salary once you become a viable asset to a radio station. The trick is becoming that "viable asset" as a radio personality. The best case scenario is one million or more per year. The worst case scenario is nothing or close to it, at least for the first couple of months. On average, a radio personality will make between $16,000 to $90,000 per year depending on the stations income, market size, your abilities and appearance money.

Remember that radio is "the entertainment business" on a smaller scale than TV, but if you decide to make radio a career, in a way, you will become "famous" and have lots of fun at work!

HARSH TRUTHS

Most people think that they have the ability to talk on the radio. Here's a fact that every radio personality knows…everyone stinks when they start! You may have the potential to be great. Even if you do a good job when you start, you will listen to a recording of your first break in two, five or ten years and laugh hysterically at yourself.

If you are thinking that the tone of your voice will propel your radio career because it is nice and deep or sensuous and sexy…you are dead wrong! There are countless DJs who sound better than Zeus and Darth Vador put together. Although this is a plus, program directors of radio stations do not care how great your voice sounds if you do not have a great personality! Anyone with a good voice who is able to press buttons and talk can be a DJ. DJs are the guys/girls who make announcements and play music at clubs, weddings, parties and bat mitzvahs. *Personalities* entertain you between the music and announcements.

From now on, for the purposes of your education in radio, we will be referring to DJs as *on-air personalities.* You will be referred to as a *personality* inside the business and that's exactly what you are hired to provide for the audience.

Don't be mistaken into thinking that you have to be overly outrageous, hilarious or scream and yell to be a great radio personality. You simply need to be yourself. Here is the question that will tell you whether you can be successful on the air; do you have friends and do your friends like to be around you? If you answered "yes," then you have a great chance. When you become a radio personality, listeners will like you for the same reason your friends like you, your personality! There are just a lot more people getting to know you once you are on the radio. Just remember that there will always be a few who don't like your sense of humor, story telling and personality. Don't let that bother you. When you start working on the air, be yourself and you will be accepted by the majority of listeners.

THE CLEAR CHANNEL EFFECT

Twenty years ago many radio stations were individually owned and companies who owned several stations were much smaller. The biggest change in radio happened when former president Bill Clinton signed the telecommunications act of 1996. The legislation virtually eliminated the national limit on station ownership. Clear Channel quickly went on a shopping spree buying two of the largest radio owners in the country, Jacor and AM/FM. This gave Clear Channel control of 70 percent of the radio market and approximately 1,182 stations in 2003. Clear Channel also acquired the NexGen/Profit computer program and networked the system throughout all of their radio stations in the country. The *voice tracking* feature on the Profit system and the network to other Clear Channel stations meant that one on-air personality employed by Clear Channel could work at four separate stations anywhere in the country and sound like they were "live."

This is when the "blood bath" began and personalities all over the country were getting fired by Clear Channel. Clear Channels salary saving scheme went into effect by keeping their "star personalities" in larger markets and having them voice track shows in other markets. They pay the personality one third of the salary for that market and it only takes one hour of recording time per day. For example, an on-air personality has a "live" 4 hour show in San Diego, resides there and gets paid $40,000 a year. After his/her shift, they spend one hour recording another 4 hour shift and then send it to a station in Salt Lake City to run the next day. That personality gets one third of the salary that the Salt Lake City job would pay, which adds another $8,000 to his/her salary. That personality also voice tracks for two other stations in different markets and gets one third of those salaries. Now one personality is making $64,000 a year and doing the job of four people. Clear Channel just saved roughly $66,000 in salaries that year and eliminated 3 jobs.

Even program directors, promotion directors, production directors, traffic managers, sales staff and general managers now have to oversee 4 stations in a single market instead of one. This means personalities were not the only ones getting fired. In a nutshell, Clear Channel eliminated about 3 out of every 4 radio jobs out of the stations that they owned and raised the salaries of the now, over worked surviving staff members.

This whole greed driven fiasco was the reason that independently owned radio stations started educating the listeners about Clear Channel, criticizing "corporate radio" and adopting the popular "independent radio" monikers.

By the way, at a recent NAB (National Association of Broadcasters) convention in Las Vegas, keynote speaker and former president Bill Clinton, apologized to the audience for signing the telecommunications act of 1996, after realizing the carnage he had caused.

THE CURRENT STATE OF RADIO

Local radio stations have had to survive devastating ratings drops in recent years due to the popularity of CDs, iPods, TVs in cars and especially, satellite radio (Sirius and XM). This does not mean that there is not a future in becoming an on-air personality. Although there is a fluctuating growth of subscribers and satellite radio is gaining listeners, not everyone is or will continue to be a fan of satellite radio. If satellite radio continues to grow, you could always consider working for XM or Sirius after gaining experience.

Radio stations have already seen the effect of CDs, iPods, and TVs in cars and although the ratings have dipped, the stations have survived and are making plenty of money. It still remains to be seen what kind of effect satellite radio will have on local "terrestrial" radio stations. The belief is that there will always be people who will not want to pay the monthly fee and/or equipment costs for satellite radio and most listeners still want to be updated on traffic, news, entertainment and contests from local stations.

Each station used to need at least 6 full time personalities and about 6 part time personalities. Because of the Clear Channel effect there are definitely fewer jobs than there were 10 years ago, but DON'T WORRY. Most of the out of work personalities have moved on to other careers and new talent is few and far between. The good news is that there is plenty of room for new talent if you are good enough. There is still an abundance new job postings every day on industry websites which is promising. If all of these factors were bankrupting local radio stations, we would not be seeing these daily job openings on a regular basis.

Regardless of the current "state of radio," talented personalities can still make tons of money in this business. All you need is the right direction and the knowledge of what steps you need to take to get there.

Now, let's get you on the air as a radio personality! Read carefully, apply what you learn and get ready for the fame, fans, fun and freebies.

GETTING STARTED

If you want to be a radio personality, you need to get started as an employee at a radio station. There are countless stories of radio personalities getting lucky, knowing the right person or who have a family member in the business. These are stories that may be true and do happen, but it is very rare for the average person.

In this book you will learn the most effective and quickest methods of getting a job "on the air" at a radio station. You will also learn valuable "radio" terminology that will make you sound like a professional and keep you proficient around the office. There will also be very important DO'S and DON'TS throughout this book assuring that you will immediately be perceived as competent in the radio community. You will also get valuable resource information that will teach you where to look for job openings and important trade magazines and websites that will help educate you on the business.

This informational book was designed to give you the most effective and relevant information in as few words as possible focusing on attaining a career as an on-air personality. You will learn the most effective ways to get your foot in the door and "on the air" in the shortest amount of time without spending thousands of dollars enrolling in a broadcasting school or spending four years in college.

After you have applied any of the "methods" of getting your foot in the door at a radio station and become an employee, apprentice or intern, it is recommended that you keep this book handy as a reference guide and refer to it as a valuable training tool in your quest to become successful in achieving an "on-air" position.

There will come a time when the experienced guidance of fellow employees along with trial and error will take over and start teaching you details of the business and you will no longer need to rely on this book to guide you as you grow into a well rounded radio personality.

Remember, radio stations are always looking for reliable promotion interns and the ***promotions department*** is where you will most likely start working. Where you go from there will depend on how closely you follow this advice and how eager you are to succeed!

RADIO TERMINOLOGY

To get the most out of this book, you will have to know some *radio terminology*. This is valuable information that will be used throughout this book and the most common terms that you will hear inside radio stations. Here you will get the most used words, definitions and some explanations of the word.

PROGRAMMING TERMS:

PROGRAMMING – Anything that has to do with what is broadcast.

TRAFFIC – Not only the term for traffic on the roads, but a department inside the radio station that schedules the time, hour and frequency of that days commercials to be played.

FORMAT – The type of content that is the broadcasting material for any particular radio station.

PRODUCTION – Every radio station has one or more "production rooms" that are used to produce commercials or station elements. Larger stations will have a production director and assistants who are required to produce all spots, the personalities are required to do the "voice over." All other stations require the personalities to know how to produce commercials. Spots will be distributed evenly amongst the on-air staff to be produced and ready to "air" by the start date. Most stations require the on-air staff to know how to produce commercials which will also be part of your job description.

AIRCHECK – A common term in radio when a personality records his/her talk breaks, usually onto cassette or CD. These are used either for the Program Director to listen and critique your work or to send to another radio stations program director to get a job on the air.

TALK BREAK – Any time you turn on the microphone and speak to the audience.

HITTING THE POST – This refers to personalities talking over a song intro right up to the point that the vocals start. This was a big deal in the '80s and early '90s. It started as a way of keeping the momentum of the music moving forward on the station. It turned into a personality's way of showing off to his/her peers. Now, it is still widely practiced, but doesn't mean much to the average listener except that it is annoying. The latest trend is for the on air staff to respect the music and not talk over the intros.

BACK SELL – Talking about and promoting what just happened on your station. Usually, you will be back selling music so the listener knows who the artist was, *"That was the Foo Fighters and DOA on Q-102."*

FRONT SELL – Talking about and promoting what is coming up on your station. You can front sell a station promotion, a song, a traffic situation, etc. *"Up next, its Pearl Jam on Live 105!" "Want to go to the biggest party in town? After the break, I'll tell you where it is…on Mix 104."*

BIT – An entertaining talk break that usually consists of parodies and/or characters while focusing on current events, news stories and other topical subjects. Morning shows do lots of bits.

INTROS – This is the beginning of a song that is instrumental and plays before the singing starts. Also known as a "ramp." Most personalities will use this time to talk while the intro is playing. Some stations encourage this practice and others are adamant about "respecting the music" and do not want you to talk over the intro of songs.

MUSIC BEDS – A music bed is instrumental music which is used to play while the personality is talking on the air. A bed is usually used on music stations to keep the sound and rhythm of the station flowing while the personality talks. Music beds are also used to produce spots. Notice how a commercial on the radio almost always has music playing underneath. Every radio station has a wide variety of music beds for you to use.

DAYPARTING – When a music director or program director plays a certain song or program at a certain time of day because it is more fitting. Heavy, fast upbeat songs are usually played at night because it matches the listener's energy level.

TIME SLOT/SHIFT – The on air personality's scheduled time to be on the air.

SPOT – The "inside" word for commercial.

SFX – Short for "sound effects." Sound effects are used everywhere on a radio station! Radio does not have the luxury of being able to use pictures like TV, so sound effects take the place of pictures helping to give the listener a "mental picture" of what they are hearing. You will see sound effects placed strategically in written commercial copy (tire screech, crying baby, door opening). Sound effects are also used in almost all sweepers and drops (lasers, zaps, beeps). Every station has an extensive library of SFX.

IMAGING – Every radio and TV station has a "station voice" that creates an image for that particular station. This is the voice that you will hear whenever the personality does not talk, whether it is between music or in and out of the stop sets.

STOP SET – When the music or "programming" stops and commercials are played. You are likely to hear this in a studio, *"How many spots are in this stop set?"*

SWEEPER – A "sweeper" is a short produced station imaging tool that is voiced by the stations imaging person and plays between songs for identification. A sweeper's sole purpose is to make sure that you are aware of what station you are listening to and what they are currently doing. *"You're inside 40 minutes of non-stop rock...on ROCK 105.3 FM!"*

DROP – A "drop" is like a sweeper, but is most often shorter and used to promote a personality or an artist. *"Howard Stern (sfx) on Sirius satellite radio!"*

PLAYLIST – A list of the day's music either on paper for the on air staff to play physically or inserted into the computer system which plays the music automatically. It's true, radio stations rarely take requests!

CLOCK – Obviously, you know what a clock is. In radio terms, "the clock" is not only a clock, but a written diagram of a real clock used as a standard guide for every personality to obey. This will show you what time you are to talk, what you are reading, when to play spots and how long your music sweeps are. "Clocks" are becoming primitive, but will be used if the station does not rely on a computer.

REMOTE – Broadcasting from a location outside of the studio, usually an advertiser's place of business.

APPEARANCES – When a personality is required to "appear" at a location for a pre-determined period of time, to attract customers. This requires you to be well informed about the business and location, dressed in station attire, shake hands, play games, answer questions, provide call-ins or phoners to the radio station and provide MC (Master of Ceremony) services.

LINERS – There are two kinds of liners, "written" and "recorded." Written liners are to be talked about live by the personality, usually right before a stop set. Liners are commonly information about station remotes, promotions and contests. Recorded liners are produced and are usually scheduled to play before or after a stop set. Because it's recorded, the personality does not have to talk about it live, but he/she MUST play the recorded version.

PSAs – Since radio stations sell "air" and everyone owns the "air" every radio station must allocate a certain amount of time each year for Public Service Announcements. Complaints to the FCC about your stations non-cooperation by public service organizations could get the stations license revoked. PSAs are either read live by the personality or are recorded like liners.

RATINGS TERMS:

ARBITRON – The ratings company who sends radio listeners a diary to keep track of what station they are listening to at any given time. Although Arbitron is completely inaccurate, this is the last word on how many people are listening to your station and how much radio stations can justly charge advertisers. Commonly referred to as *"The Book."*

MARKET SIZE – The city and population of the city in which a radio station is located in the United States.

DEMO – Or "Demographic." The age and sex of a listener.

TECHNICAL TERMS:

CONTROL BOARD – This is the cockpit of a radio station where all volumes and events are controlled by the on air staff. You will need some training on "the board" before the Program Director even considers letting you go on the air. Although very intimidating at first, keep a close eye on an experienced on air personality at work, ask questions and pay attention!!! You may be surprised at how quick and easy learning to "run a board" can be.

POT – NO! Not that. A pot is referred to as any one of the many volume controls on a "control board." *"Pot that up, it's not loud enough."*

CUE BUTTON – On every control board there are many volume controls or "POTS." At the bottom of each "POT" there is a cue button. When the cue button is engaged and the "POT" is turned down you are able to listen to the audio through the in studio speaker without it playing on the air. *"I need to hear that in cue before it airs."*

AUTOMATION – Just like any other company that relies on computers to do the majority of work for them (assembly line, banking, etc.) Radio stations have entered the computer age as well. Computer programs like Profit, Scott Studios and RCS do all of the work for you. The music director inserts the music, the traffic director inserts the spots, the program or promotion director inserts the recorded promos and liners and it runs itself. Your job is to talk, answer phones and have no excuses for not being prepared because "automation" has created lots of free time for the modern personality.

VOICE-TRACKING – One of the money saving features for radio stations across the country and the reason that every out of work personality in America despises Clear Channel who owns Profit systems, the most widely used automation program in the nation for radio stations. Voice tracking is a feature that all automation systems have, but Profit has the most user friendly version which allows a personality to pre-record a whole show in less than an hour. The profit system automatically plays your voice tracks when you tell it to without skipping a beat. A co-worker will have to teach you how to voice-track, but when you get to that point, I assure you, it's a must know.

CART – Carts used to mean "cartridges." Carts looked like 8-Track tapes that played spots, sweepers and sometimes music. You will probably not encounter a cart at this point, but the term "cart" is still used to describe storage walls on the computer programs that you will be using, commonly referred to as *"cart walls."*

MICROWAVE – A relay system that radio stations use to shoot the signal from the broadcast studios to the tower. Without Microwave systems every radio station would have to broadcast from the tower site.

STICK – The slang word for "broadcast tower."

EAS TEST – By law The Emergency Alert System is required to be installed and in working order at EVERY radio and TV station in operation per the FCC. Legally a station must test the system periodically by simply pressing a button located on the EAS device. When you are hired for an on air shift, the program director will inform you about the location of this button and when it is to be activated.

LEGAL TERMS:

FCC – Federal Communications Commission. The police for any business that broadcasts any material.

CALL LETTERS – These are the stations legal call letters given at licensing. Call letters always start with *W* or *K* in the U.S. and have a total of four letters. Radio stations usually try to use the call letters as an acronym for the stations moniker. *"KROQ, The World Famous K-ROCK."*

CLUSTER – A "cluster" is a group of radio stations that are owned by the same person or company. There can be a cluster of 2 stations or 2000 stations.

RADIO STATION DEPARTMENTS/TITLES

1. PROGRAMMING

Program Director – PD
Assistant Program Director – APD
Music Director – MD
Production Director
News Department
On Air Staff

2. SALES:

General Sales Manager – GSM
National Sales Manager
Regional Sales Manager

Local Sales Manager
Sales Staff

3. ENGINEERING:

Chief Engineer
Studio Engineers
Maintenance Engineers

4. BUSINESS:

Business Manager
Traffic Manager
Accounting
Personnel
Promotions Director
Promotions Staff

The general manager or GM is in charge of all departments but concentrates on long-range planning and
management decisions. Most day-to-day decisions are
made by the heads of the four key station departments:
the program director, general sales manager, chief
engineer and business manager.

RADIO STATION FORMATS

Active Rock
Adult Alternative
Adult Contemporary
Adult Standards
Alternative
CHR – Contemporary Hit Radio
CHR/Pop
CHR/Rhythmic
Classical
Classic Rock
Country
Hot AC
NAC/Smooth Jazz
News/Talk
Oldies/Classic Rock

Religious/Gospel
R&B
Spanish
Top 40
Urban
Urban AC

GETTING YOUR FOOT IN THE DOOR

METHOD 1 (THE COLLEGE INTERN)

If you are taking communication classes at your college they will either have a college radio station where you can learn the "basics" or your college will have connections to local radio stations for students to earn work credits for the course they are taking. This brings us to your first avenue of entry into a radio station.

IF YOU HAVE THE OPPORTUNITY, WORK AT THE COLLEGE STATION SHORTLY FOR EXPERIENCE AND PUT IT ON YOUR RESUME, BUT DON'T EXPECT THIS TO IMPRESS A NON-COLLEGE RADIO EMPLOYER.

USE THE COLLEGE CONNECTIONS TO GET A JOB AS AN INTERN AT A LOCAL RADIO STATION.

You may already know about this method of entry into a radio station, but what you don't know is that radio stations are not always thrilled to hire college interns! This is because they know that you are working there to earn credits and most students only do as much as needed in order to pass the class and move on. This is where most students go wrong who are looking for a serious career in radio broadcasting. They think that when they have graduated or completed the class, the radio jobs will be abundant because of their college training and because of the experience they gained by working at an actual radio station. In reality, this is the chance of a lifetime where most interns miss out on a major opportunity.

Once you have been hired as an intern here is a list of tactics that will separate you from the other interns and show management that you are interested in more than just college credits.

DO'S AND DON'T'S

- BE INTERESTED IN MORE THAN YOUR ASSIGNED DUTIES.
- SPEND MUCH OF YOUR FREE TIME AT THE STATION.

- GET TO KNOW THE DEPARTMENT HEADS.
- BE NICE AND EASY GOING.
- ASK QUESTIONS BUT DO NOT BE
  ANNOYING.
- DO NOT COMPLAIN!!!

You will not believe how responsive management will be to someone who is eager to learn more than is required of them as an intern.

If you follow these rules as an intern, management WILL notice and as soon as there is an opening you could be next in line as a paid employee.

GETTING YOUR FOOT IN THE DOOR

METHOD 2 (APPRENTICESHIP)

If you are not in college and do not plan on attending college, don't worry. You can still get a job a radio station and thrive if you have common sense and a strong work ethic. Many radio personalities are not college graduates and got their start by "knocking on doors." Although radio stations do not commonly refer to this as an apprenticeship, that's really what it is. You are offering your services for free or for little pay in order to learn the business. You will have to convince the Program Director or the Promotions Director to give you a chance to "prove" yourself. If it is obvious that you are "hungry" to learn, they WILL be interested in hiring you. Make no mistake; this can be a bit painful for a while. You will have to do all of the dirty work until you become an asset. The good news is that it will not take very long to become an asset if you use the same tactics as we mentioned in "the method 1" section.

DO'S AND DON'T'S

- BE INTERESTED IN MORE THAN YOUR ASSIGNED DUTIES.
- SPEND MUCH OF YOUR FREE TIME AT THE STATION.
- GET TO KNOW THE DEPARTMENT HEADS.
- BE NICE AND EASY GOING.
- ASK QUESTIONS BUT DO NOT BE ANNOYING.
- DO NOT COMPLAIN!!!

If you follow these rules and do a good job, you will get noticed by one or all of the department heads and most likely offered a paid job in the department in which you are most needed.

This can take anywhere from two weeks to six months. If it takes longer, it's time to take it upon yourself and ask about paid employment. Since the goal is to be on the radio, it is appropriate to ask the Program

Director for a paid position. Try to not get roped into being a slave for the sales or business department throughout this process. Remember, your goal is to be on the radio and the only person who will make that happen is the Program Director. Programming is the department that you want to work in!

GETTING YOUR FOOT IN THE DOOR

METHOD 3 (THE EAGER/TALENTED LISTENER)

This may sound unbelievable, but it works! Be a dedicated fan of the station in which you are trying gain employment. Listen to the station as often as possible, know the contests, call in for contests, call in for games, help the personality with bits, be excited, be entertaining and PLAY ALONG! Radio personalities are starving for competent, out spoken listeners to call in and get involved; they want people who "get it." If you are going to attempt this method of entry it is crucial that you sound competent and are well spoken, even funny. In fact, this is a good test to find out if you have any business being in this business.

Use your free time away from your day job to befriend a radio personality and be a useful listener. Call in and play along as either your witty, competent self or as a funny character. You can seal the deal by showing up at the station remotes and getting to know the staff and even the all important Program Director! Once the staff gets to know you, trusts you and knows that you are "normal," you will have a good chance of becoming "the lucky listener."

Many listeners have become on-air personalities by default using this method than any other! You may be a non-paid employee for a short while and it may take some time to gain the trust of the staff, but once you do, a station is more than willing to quickly teach you the basics and put you on the air part time as a co-host or as an intern until you know the ropes.

In the eyes of a program director, a person who has "natural talent" with no radio experience can be just as valuable as someone with radio experience. Here are the rules to keep in mind when using this method.

DON'T WEAR OUT YOUR WELCOME! ONCE A WEEK IS THE MOST THAT YOU SHOULD CALL TO PARTICIPATE. EVEN IF YOU ARE AN ENTERTAINING LISTENER, THE

Personality Can Only Use You So Much Before It Becomes Obvious That He/She Is Relying On You For Material And Becomes Annoying To The Other Listeners. It Also Will Start To Sound Like You Are The Stations Only Listener.

Only Call A Station When You Are Prompted By The Personality. He/She Has Lots Of Calls To Take And Does Not Want To Chit Chat!

Be Cordial, Well Dressed And Well Spoken When You Show Up At A Personality's Appearance. Don't Consume All Of His/Her Time In Pointless Conversation, But If He/She Is Not Busy, This Is The Time To Chit Chat.

Most Importantly…Don't Ask For Free Stuff!!! This Will Immediately Categorize You As Just Another Greedy Listener And Prevent You From Getting Your Foot In The Door

Following these rules will get you noticed as the "cool listener." Most likely, you will not be "lucky" enough to start on the air right away. Even though you are talented, you will have to put some work into this method, push the process along and pay some dues to become the "lucky" listener.

Once the personality trusts you, he/she will introduce you to the program director at an event. This is exactly what you want to happen! Go to one more event where the personality you know is working. This time, create small talk with the program director. If the PD is receptive to a short conversation, use the following questions and comments to peak their interest and "stroke" their ego. (Choose two or three of the following, any more and they will start to catch on and you will seem over-anxious).

COMMENTS:

I love your radio station.

This station is so much better than your competitor (use competitors name).

It's nice to meet the person in charge of my favorite radio station.

QUESTIONS:

Can I take a tour of the station sometime?

How long have you been in radio?

Where else have you worked in radio?

Remember to be sincere and genuinely interested in their station and accomplishments. People in radio are very dedicated to this business and are dying to share their knowledge and background with anyone who is interested. Now you have a personal connection with the all important program director!

It is now time to get a business card from the personality and/or the program director and call for a tour ASAP. Even though someone else will probably be giving you the tour, this could be your first opportunity to discuss your interest in an internship or apprenticeship! If you do not get the chance to talk to the personality or the PD, call them after a couple of days and let them know that you loved what you saw on the tour and are interested in working there. From start to finish, this method of entry may take a few months, but will lead to an interview with the promotions department or program director and get you your first radio job if you are eager enough. Follow the DO'S and DON'T'S in methods 1 and 2 after you get your intern or apprenticeship and you will be well on your way to a paid position!

GETTING YOUR FOOT IN THE DOOR

METHOD 4 (THE AIRCHECK TAPE)

Aside from the "methods" we have already discussed, on air personalities who have experience get jobs by sending a resume and aircheck to the program director of a radio station. Although this will get you on the air right away, you will have to send out tens to hundreds of airchecks before you get a job, especially if you are lacking "on-air" experience. If you are lucky enough to find interest, it will likely be in a very small market and you will have to relocate and survive on a very small wage for a while.

There are several ways to put together your first aircheck. Without experience, you will have to spend some money to make your aircheck as professional as possible. The following is a list of the best ways to arm you with a quality aircheck tape for job mailings.

Find a local "production house/sound studio" that rents out studio time. Most studios will provide an engineer/sound editor who will put the aircheck together for you as part of the rental agreement. Write out 5 talk breaks that are anywhere from 10 seconds to 60 seconds long using a fictional radio station. Practice delivering the breaks so that you will get it right the first time and you will not have to pay again to re-do your aircheck. Bring songs on CD that you want to use as the format, (you will only be using the beginning and end of the songs. The PD wants to hear you, not the music. The engineer/sound editor should know this). If the studio does not have a duplication service, use the CD burner on your computer or find a duplicating service and make as many copies as you need. Label the CD'S with your name and phone number. Put your CD in a jewel case and send to the desired station with your current resume and a short cover letter (5 sentences, at the most). Airchecks should only be 3 to 5 minutes in duration.

If you have access to your college radio station, ask a student or teacher to help you put together an aircheck in the stations production room. If you do not have access to the station, offer to pay a student to help you while keeping the above rules in mind.

After applying one of the first three "methods" of getting your foot in the door, start creating a relationship with the production director of the radio station. Keep him/her informed of your interest in being a radio personality. If you go out of your way to be nice and/or helpful to the production director, they will feel compelled to help you in their spare time and give you all of the information you need to put a quality aircheck together. If you are already an employee at the station, you want to use this aircheck to get on the air by giving the finished product to your stations PD for critiquing. You may have to learn the art of production and keep trying, as the PD most likely, will not like what they hear the first time.

We have listed this option and you are free to try getting your first job by putting together an aircheck, but it is not recommended until you have spent some time working at a radio station and have had a chance to ask your PD and/or the on-air staff for an example of a professional aircheck. You can also get a better idea of a professional aircheck by ordering real airchecks of seasoned pro's from a company called California Airchecks. They are on the web at www.californiaaircheck.com.

SEARCHING FOR THE RIGHT RADIO STATION

Now that you have learned the most effective methods of how to get your foot in the door, you need to decide which "method of entry" is best suited for you and find a radio station in which to work and apply your knowledge. This is not the time to be picky about the format or the popularity of a radio station when pursuing an internship or apprenticeship. Remember that you do not yet have experience and you may have to compromise on the caliber of the radio station. You should certainly start at the top of your list and work your way down, but the goal is to get experience!

Here are some facts that may help you decide which station to pursue:

The larger the market, ratings, popularity and reputation of a radio station…The harder it is to get your foot in the door and get on the air, but you will learn more in less time, you will be trained very well and have a great credit on your resume for future jobs.

The smaller the market, ratings, popularity and reputation of a radio station…The easier it is to get your foot in the door and get on the air, but you will learn less in more time, you will be trained poorly and have a less impressive resume for future jobs.

If you are familiar with your local radio stations you can find addresses in the yellow pages under "advertising" or by searching online, (yellowpages.com, google.com, etc. key word; radio stations). There are also many radio websites that have job listings all over the country. Many of these listings will not be in your market, but if you don't mind relocating, these listings will give you more options. There is a list of the most useful and resourceful radio websites in the "Industry Websites" section of this book. Right now, concentrate on choosing a radio station in your area. Even though this will narrow down your options, be assured that radio stations are always looking for dedicated employees who are eager to be loyal, hard working and learn the business! Using these methods work, but it does not always come easy. You may have to politely push harder than you anticipated convincing a station of your worth and dedication.

FINDING RADIO STATIONS

You now know the easiest ways to get a job on the radio. You now know to start inquiring about an intern or apprenticeship at one of your local stations. What you don't know are the exact resources that will guide you to the right station for an intern or apprenticeship. Some of this has been discussed, but let's get into some detail. You have read and hopefully understand the first part of this book. If you truly want to have a job on the air, the first step is to have a list of every radio station in your area. The phone book may not have all stations listed and you may not find a complete list online, but there is a book that has a list of every radio station in the country including your town. Not only does it have a list of all the radio stations, it has phone numbers, addresses, owners, program directors, format and anything else that you need to know. This book is called *the radio yearbook* and it is available at almost every library in the country. You are not allowed to take the book from the library, but you can make copies of all of the radio stations in your area. You can also buy the book from amazon.com or nabstore.com. You probably don't realize how many radio stations are in your area until you take a look at *the radio yearbook*. Now you can take advantage of every opportunity your market has to offer and, if you want, knock on every door. As the title says, this book is only printed once a year, so some material may be outdated. Use the phone numbers to call the radio stations that interest you and confirm that the information is current. Then start doing your best to set up appointments with the program directors. If you can not get them on the phone ask the receptionist for the program director's email address. Most people, including program directors prefer communicating through email. If they won't give you an email address, show up at the station and express your interest face to face with the program director. This may take guts and a few attempts for some people, but there are many success stories of personalities getting their first job by being politely persistent.

THE SECRET

The secret to landing your first job is simple. If you saw a trend in the first three methods, you have caught on! Interns and apprentices are non-paid positions. You will also get little to no pay if you are the lucky listener and this is why method 4 is not recommended for a beginner. The first three methods are all based on the secret and the secret is how almost every radio personality got their first job. Here is *the secret* that has started countless careers for on air personalities and is the first lesson in "paying your dues." **YOU MUST BE WILLING TO WORK FOR FREE**. This is the only sure way to gain instant employment with no experience. It is very difficult to get your first job at a radio station if you are not willing to make this sacrifice. By offering to work for no pay you are really proving your ambition and commitment to learning this business and it is virtually impossible for a radio station to turn down this offer. This is why being an intern, apprentice or lucky listener is highly recommended. If you just sighed in frustration and disappointment of having to work for free, you are not alone. No one wants to do this. Unless you are willing to move to a very small town for very little pay, you are likely going to have to start with no pay. If you refuse to work for free or relocate to a small town for little money, you may as well close this book right now and choose another career path.

If you are still reading, there is good news. In the radio industry, there is an abundance of laziness and carefree attitudes from non-paid employees. Like we mentioned in the first two methods of getting your foot in the door, hard work and dedication gets rewarded very quickly! I have seen non-paid employees get on the payroll within a week. I have also seen many lazy non-paid employees get fired to make room for a new intern or apprentice with a strong work ethic. Remember that even if you are offering your services for free there is always a chance that the station is fully staffed and happy with the employees. Just move on to the next station on your list and try again. In many cases, offering to work for free is your ticket in and being reliable, hard working and dedicated will get you paid very quickly. Once again, it will not be very long until you are put on the payroll if you are an asset.

OFFICE CONDUCT/POSITIVE BEHAVIOR

The goal of this book and the reason this book was written is to get a beginner on the air as soon as possible. Here are some DO'S that could get you on the air and on the payroll within a month and some DON'T'S that could get you fired within a day.

DO'S:

DO be humble, genuine, honest and positive.

DO ask relevant questions and LEARN.

DO be willing to help whether it's lifting, cleaning, errands, etc.

DO ask if you don't know how to do something. They know you are learning and they will help you when you need it.

DO be on time for work.

DO create a friendly relationship with the person-alities and management. They will start wanting to help you reach your goals.

DONT'S:

DON'T start getting an attitude or acting like a know it all. This is not tolerated!

DON'T steal from the stations prize closet. More interns get fired for this than anything else! If you ask for something; t-shirt, CD, concert tickets, key chain, etc. you will likely get an OK.

DON'T wander into the on-air studio and chat with the personality or ask for a request to be played!

DON'T drink, smoke, have sex (yes, it happens) or joy ride in a station vehicle. Although some of this may be ignored and laughed at, it is not a smart career move.

DON'T be late for work.

DON'T back stab or talk behind your co-workers backs. You never know who is in-cahoots with man-agement.

DON'T be rude to listeners, either on location or in the office. Listeners are the life-blood of the station. If management catches wind of this type of behavior there will be serious repercussions.

TRANSITIONING FROM PROMOTIONS TO PROGRAMMING

Hopefully, you have used the secret, applied one of the four methods of getting your foot in the door and you are now working at a radio station. You may even be getting paid and you are working in close proximity to the program director, the personalities and the production director. You should be about 2 to 6 months in and have proven yourself as a dedicated and hard working employee. It is time to start letting these folks in on your intentions of being a radio personality and to start asking what you can do to make this happen. If you have taken the advice of this book, you are in good standing and they are willing to give you a break. It is now crucial that you learn the basics!

Approach the PD and ask him/her if one of the personalities can teach you how to run the board, learn the computer automation system, read for a commercial or assist a personality during their shift. If you are always there when needed and they are happy with your performance, you can start transitioning into full time help for one of the personalities, production director or the program director.

If you are working in the promotions department, the promotions director will not be happy about this. This is because he/she will be losing a good employee and now realizes that they just got used in your pursuit of an on-air position. This is normal. While this process happening, you should still be loyal and continue working in the promotions department so that there is not a feeling of betrayal. If you have been pleasant, hard working and loyal, the PD and promotions director will find a way to accommodate your wishes.

This is a time that could also turn into a crossroads for you. If your intentions to be a personality are not well received and it is clear that they will not give you a chance, you may have to decide whether it is worth your time to stick around hoping that they will change their minds. It is up to you. You can put in more time and hope they have a change of heart or start interviewing at other stations. Although it may be discouraging to seek employment at another radio station and it may set you back a couple of months, you will find that your experience will move you along much faster at your next job. If your request is well received, it is time to take advantage of your good fortune and hard work. Whether you start getting trained by a personality or you are assigned to be the production director's right hand man, YOU ARE IN! Pay attention, listen and learn! This is the time that you will receive your most valuable information which you will use for the rest of your career.

WHAT YOU NEED TO LEARN BEFORE AN ON-AIR SHIFT

You are now working in programming even if you still have some obligations to the promotions department. Whether you are assisting the production director, the program director or a personality, you are paying attention, listening and learning! You are much more educated on the inner workings of the radio business and now getting trained by a professional about programming duties. You don't want to hear this, but you will have to do this for a while until you feel confident about doing your first on-air shift. In addition, the program director will be paying attention to your progress and taking note of any feed back about your performance. Here are the things that you should be learning at this stage.

WORKING WITH THE PRODUCTION DIRECTOR:

How to do voice-overs for spots.

How to run the production control board.

How to edit using the stations sound editing program.

How to enter pre-produced spots into the computer for airing.

How to retrieve pre-produced spots from the internet, from emails and from the DGS system.

WORKING WITH THE PROGRAM DIRECTOR:

How to schedule music.

How to read and understand Arbitron and the ratings system.

Philosophies about the business aspects of programming.

WORKING WITH A RADIO PERSONALITY:

How to run the on-air control board.

How the phone system works.

How to use the phone editing system (360, Profit, Voxpro, etc.).

How to run the on-air computer system (RCS, Profit, Scott Studios, etc.).

How to properly screen phone calls.

How to put together an aircheck.

GETTING YOUR FIRST ON-AIR SHIFT

You are ready to do it, go on the air for the first time! You have paid some dues and you are knowledgeable about details that you needed to know about the promotions, production and programming departments. You have built relationships with the right people and they have faith in you because they trained you.

It is time to do whatever you can, legally and morally to convince the program director to let you work a fill-in or overnight on-air shift. By now, they should know that this is your goal and will reward you very soon. This will have a lot to do with the timing, your tactics and circumstances. This is an important time to be able to read the program director's mind and approach him/her when they are in a good mood!

Remember, you can not get this accomplished in one day. It may take a few weeks once you ask for a shift. You may also have to be politely persistent to get your first on-air shift. You will have the best shot of getting on the air during a holiday when other personalities are on vacation or have the day off. It is also a good idea to have an on-air personality put in a good word for you. Hopefully at this point, you have had assistance from the production director or a personality in putting together an aircheck tape for the program director to hear and critique. If the PD has few criticisms about your performance, they will do their best to get you on somehow.

This is why you have spent time at a radio station, this is why you volunteered your time and this is why you asked questions and learned! You WILL get on the air if you have shown your eagerness and ambition. Now get ready to have the most thrilling, nerve racking and accomplished feeling you will ever experience…going on the air for the first time!

GOLDEN RULES FOR THE RADIO PERSONALITY

These are fundamental rules that you MUST know and apply to insure success of your first shift. These rules will also help you throughout your career and will bring out the best of your abilities as an on-air personality.

Read this next part very carefully! Always keeping these rules in mind can shave years off of your climb to the top as a radio personality. You will also want to use these rules for your first on-air shift as they will help you perform more professionally.

BE YOURSELF – It usually takes years for a personality to try and figure out who they want to be on the radio. In the end, they all come to the same conclusion…"All I had to do was BE MYSELF!" A personality can get ten years into their career wondering what took them so long to discover this secret. If you take anything from this book, take this advice, hold it close and NEVER forget it! Here it is again, BE YOURSELF! Like we mentioned earlier, there is a reason that you have friends, there is a reason you are loved, there is a reason people like to be around you. It is because you are YOU and that is exactly who you want to be on the radio. This does not mean that you should be timid, boring, vulgar or anything that is negative just because that is your personality. You need to let the positive aspects of your personality shine bright on the air!

TALK TO ONE PERSON – Always keep a mental picture in your head of ONE person that you are speaking to. It could be a past love, a sibling, your mother, your father, Pamela Anderson, Richard Gere or even God. It doesn't matter, just pick one person and talk to them when you are on the radio! Doing this will make you sound very conversational and real, like you are hanging out with your buddy. If you think about talking to your whole audience, you will come off sounding fake like an announcer or you may sound like you are reading.

HAVE SOMETHING TO SAY – There will be times when you are scheduled to talk but you have nothing planned or scheduled and you end up fumbling words and saying something irrelevant or stupid. You MUST plan your talk breaks. Be prepared to make sense and say something relevant, especially when you are beginning. The best advice for beginners is to write down what you are going to say word for word and practice a few times off the air. Just remember to say it like you are talking and not like you are reading! This will safe guard you from any major screw-ups.

KEEP IT SIMPLE – Have you ever heard the saying, "less is more?" This is a golden rule for radio personalities! It is not very effective when a radio personality throws so much information and details at you that you can't make heads or tails of what they just said. You have probably found yourself rolling your eyes, sighing in boredom or even changing the station because of long winded personalities. Elaborating only works if it's a very funny bit or an entertaining story. It does not work for factual information. Simple is safe and less is more.

CREATE A MENTAL PICTURE FOR THE LISTENER – Don't just talk. Give your listeners a mental picture of what you are saying. If you create a lasting image for the listener to look at, they will retain the information and start getting involved and excited about the promotion. Let's say that the station is giving away a brand new sports car. You can simply give out the information…" Caller 10 gets a chance to win that brand new $38,000 sports car." Or you can create a picture…" When I got to test drive this car I buckled up, grabbed the race inspired steering wheel, looked at all of the high tech gauges and stepped on the gas. I got forced back into the leather seat and I felt like a race car driver. Caller ten qualifies for this brand new $38,000 jet black rocket!"

DON'T TRY TO BE A COMEDIAN – You may not be as funny as you think. You were not hired to be a stand up comedian. If you think of something funny to say, you had better be darn sure that it's funny! If you absolutely have to say it, at least try it out on a co-worker so that you don't fall flat on your face. It is okay to be comical on the radio if that is your personality. Just make sure that your comedic abilities are not a fantasy in your own head before you take on the roll of the "funny" radio personality.

BLOCK OUT YOUR SURROUNDINGS – There will always be employees, guests, friends and listeners walking in and out of the studio. A radio personality's job can be a bit embarrassing for the beginner. How many people sit alone in a room and have lengthy conversations with themselves? To be able to do your best, you are going to have to put aside your inhibitions and perform. Studio visitors have a tendency to freeze and stare at you while you are talking on the radio. Don't let this throw you off and make you lose your concentration. They freeze because they know that they need to be quiet and they are staring because they either find your job interesting or have nothing else to look at. Don't let this hinder your performance, stay focused and block them out!

SOUND COMPETENT – Even if you are not educated, you must sound intelligent! Keep up on current events, pop culture and try to know a little bit about everything. If you are working for a music station, it is also imperative that you educate yourself on the artists that you play. You will be expected to know a lot about the music that you are playing every day. The music is the star! You are there to compliment the music with facts, entertainment and your personality!

NO PUKING – This is the most important NO, NO in the modern radio industry. Puking is slang for "over enunciating." It is also categorized as using your "DJ" voice or trying to sound like a "DJ." Although you need to speak clearly and enunciate properly, DO NOT PUKE! Puking is old school, unnecessary and hard to take seriously. You will be known as the station "fool" if you puke. Ask about it at a radio station, you will get several entertaining verbal examples of the definition.

TRAINING YOURSELF

Whether you are working on the air or not, there is a great way of practicing and polishing your "on-air" skills that is free, easy and very effective! You can practice in your car or at home by simply listening to a radio station and repeating after the personality who is on the air. Being in a major market is a plus because you will be listening to a radio personality who has had quality training and polished techniques in their delivery. Make sure you listen during the day as these are the personalities with the most skills and training.

Simply repeating after the personality that you are listening to out loud will teach you how to talk to the audience properly.

You can start by repeating the same thing they say. Talk as they talk, use the same inflections, energy level and style. When you get comfortable in doing this, start to tie in your personality. Use inflections, energy level and style that you are comfortable with and fits your personality. Think of things to say that will make your personality shine on the radio, as if you are actually working. This may sound ridiculous to some people, but hopefully you can realize the benefit that this will have in your performance when you get a job on the air.

Make sure that you are listening to a radio personality that has talent and experience or you may do yourself more harm than good. There are lots of inexperienced radio personalities who are working and may not be a good example of proper execution.

Call it what you want; mimicking, aping, copying or repeating, but using this method of training yourself works very well if you are listening to a well trained and talented personality. While you use this method of practicing, try to picture yourself in front of a microphone in the studio to build confidence and get used to the studio environment.

As we mentioned earlier, purchasing some airchecks of well known and professional personalities from www.californiaaircheck.com and using this training technique would be the most beneficial way of quickly improving.

SOME LAST MINUTE ADVICE

COMPETITION – Like any office environment, the on-air staff of radio stations can be very competitive. It is quite common for personalities to compete for better shifts, more money, appearances and ratings. You may encounter some jealousy and back stabbing as you become successful in this business. Part-time personalities and interns who are aspiring to be full-time on-air personalities may try to position themselves to take your job by whatever means necessary. At the least, someone may be keeping a close eye on you, ready to pounce by quietly informing the PD of any wrong-doings. This is not a common practice, but something that you are very likely to encounter in the span of your career. Always be aware of fellow employee's motives during conversations and actions they display.

NETWORKING – On a positive note, here is some great advice on how to position yourself for amazing opportunities in the future. Make it a point to network and create relationships with successful radio people across the country. Email, call and get to know PD'S and personalities. Whether you ask for advice, compliment them on their achievements or just introduce yourself. By creating relationships in the radio industry, you may find that "who you know" could eventually get you that dream job in New York or Los Angeles!

Allaccess.com is also a great source of getting your name out in the radio community. Joel Denver and the staff at allaccess are very nice people and want to know about any changes in your career and any successful stunts or promotions that you perform on the air. Everyone in the radio community reads allaccess. They will start to remember your name and find out that you are a true professional. A PD may even like what he/she reads about you so much that you get a call for a job in the future.

THE PRODUCT – Never forget that YOU are the product that you are selling to radio stations and to listeners. You must always work on the product whether it is networking, polishing your skills or educating yourself so that you sound competent.

Keep your resume current and professional. Record your on air work and always have a current aircheck ready to send out in case you get fired or you want to search for a new job.

INDUSTRY WEBSITES

There are many websites dedicated to the radio industry. This is a list of the most popular and informative radio websites. They will give you updated information on everything about the radio industry. These websites are also a valuable resource in job searching. Here is a list of the most popular industry websites.

www.allaccess.com – This is the most informative and widely used website in the radio industry. You will have to register to have access to this website, but it is free and easy. Once you register, you will have endless information about the radio industry including the most updated and extensive list of the best radio jobs in the country. Once you have registered, log on and click *job market*. This is also the best website for the latest industry news.

www.radioandrecords.com – Radio and Records is not only an industry website, but a weekly trade magazine which almost every station in the country subscribes. Although a bit pricey, you can subscribe to the magazine to keep up on all aspects of the industry. An R&R magazine subscription costs about $325.00 per year. To find job openings on this website click on *resources* then *job opportunities*. This is also a great website for the latest industry news.

www.fmqb.com – FMQB is also an industry magazine which most major market radio stations subscribe. It also has extensive updated information about the radio industry. Although it is not the best resource for job openings, it usually lists higher paying jobs in larger markets. To find job openings on this website click on *job front*.

www.tvandradiojobs.com – This website has a wide variety of behind the scenes radio jobs as well as on-air jobs from small to large markets. To find job openings on this website click on *radio*.

www.newradiostar.com – This website lists a variety of websites where you can search for radio job openings.

You can broaden your search even more by using a search engine, keyword *radio jobs*.

IN REVIEW

Along with some educational information, you have been given detailed step by step instructions of how to achieve an on air position at a radio station. Here is a condensed review of the steps to be taken from start to finish.

After reading the *introduction*, *harsh truths*, *the Clear Channel effect*, *getting started* and *the current state of radio* you need to make a final decision whether or not a career in radio is right for you.

Once you have decided to continue your pursuit as a radio personality, get familiar with the *radio terminology*, *radio station departments/titles* and *radio station formats* so that you are competent and knowledgeable when you talk to potential employers.

Choose one of the four *methods of getting your foot in the door* that best suits your situation and schedule. Be ready to apply this method when you start seeking employment, paid or not.

Decide the type of radio station that you want to pursue by using the information in *searching for the right radio station*. Decide what city/market that you are interested in working. Get phone numbers, addresses and formats in the *finding radio stations* section.

Use *the secret* to immediately convince the program director that you are serious and motivated.

Find a job at a radio station by using the methods and tactics that you have learned!

Always keep the *office conduct/positive behavior* section in mind to earn trust and respect quickly.

You have gained experience to start *transitioning from promotions to programming*. Ask the program director if you can work under him/her, a personality or the production director and start letting these people know that you are interested in being on the air.

Once you are given the opportunity of working in the programming department, refer to *what you need to learn before an on air shift* and start learning everything on this list with the help of your co-workers. Being familiar with these skills is the first step. It may take a long time to get proficient at everything on this list. If you want to get on the air quickly, concentrate on learning the *on air control board* and the *on air computer system* first. You can be working on the air while perfecting the rest of these skills.

While you are learning technical skills from the programming department, most importantly, the *on air control board* and the *on air computer system*, have the production director help you put together an air check tape for the program director to critique. After the PD is happy with your air check tape ask for a late night or fill-in shift. It is wise to have anyone with some influence put in a good word for you to the PD. If you are this far along, they WILL give you a chance to be on the air.

Now it is time to learn the *golden rules for the radio personality*, practicing the method of *training yourself* and keeping in mind the *last minute advice*.

Continue to use the *industry websites* for keeping up on industry news, networking and job hunting to advance your career to the next level.

SUMMARY

We know that this book will be a valuable resource and information tool to get you started and insure success in less time as you pursue an exciting career as an on-air radio personality.

This book has given you valuable inside information that really works! As you make the decision to start a career in radio and apply these methods and tactics, you will increase your chance of success 100 fold.

Keep in mind that this book is designed to get a beginner started in a career as an on-air personality. Not every aspect of the radio business is covered in this book, only the most relevant in required knowledge and the fundamentals to get you started. There are many aspects of ratings, philosophies, techniques and technical information that are not discussed. This

is because getting your foot in the door is one of the most challenging parts of the radio business. Once you have acquired a job in radio by using this book, your co-workers will play the roll of your "technical training" and will expand your knowledge.

We feel that hands-on experience is the best broadcasting school in the country! Although broadcasting schools will give you valuable technical training and can be helpful, most of the schools job placement programs can be lacking. This book tells you how to get on the air much quicker by getting a job on your own and investing this money into your living expenses while you are getting hands-on training at a radio station of your choice. Plus, some of the information in this book could save you the heartache of spending your hard earned money if you don't like what you have heard. This is the most valuable information that you can start with and is not taught in broadcasting schools or even college.

Good luck and we'll listen for you on the air!